TEENS AND VAPING

John Allen

ReferencePoint Press®

San Diego, CA

About the Author
John Allen is a writer who lives in Oklahoma City.

For more information, contact:
ReferencePoint Press, Inc.
PO Box 27779
San Diego, CA 92198
www.ReferencePointPress.com

LIBRARY OF CONGRESS CATALOGING-IN-PUBLICATION DATA

Names: Allen, John, 1957– author.
Title: Teens and Vaping/by John Allen.
Description: San Diego, CA : ReferencePoint Press, Inc., 2020. | Includes bibliographical references and index.
Identifiers: LCCN 2019019702 (print) | LCCN 2019022374 (ebook) | ISBN 9781682827550 (hardback) | 9781682827567 (ebook)
Subjects: LCSH: Teenagers—Tobacco use—Juvenile literature. | Vaping—Juvenile literature.
Classification: LCC HV5745 .A45 2020 (print) | LCC HV5745 (ebook) | DDC 362.29/6—dc23
LC record available at https://lccn.loc.gov/2019019702
LC ebook record available at https://lccn.loc.gov/2019022374

CONTENTS

The Vaping Trend

When someone talks about juuling, usually only the teens in the room get it. Yet juuling—a less conspicuous form of vaping—has high school administrators in an uproar across the nation. Some have resorted to sending parents e-mails warning them about the dangers of so-called e-cigarettes (e for electronic). According to a recent study by the National Institutes of Health, more than one in four high school students admitted to vaping within the last year and more than 16 percent had done so in the last month. Juul, an e-cigarette that looks like a computer thumb drive, is only the latest and coolest version. It fits comfortably in the palm of the hand, for discreet usage. Some students even report vaping with a Juul in the classroom. Mil Schooley, a student in Denver, Colorado, says most of her friends rock a Juul. "I wanna say like 50 or 60 percent?" she says. "I don't know. Maybe it's just the people I know. All my friends in college have one. It just blew up over the summer."[1]

A Controversial Product

Many teenagers today consider electronic cigarettes to be a cooler, safer, techno version of smoking. They call e-cigarettes by many different names, such as mods, vapes, vape pens, smokeless cigs, and e-hookahs. The basic e-cigarette is a battery-operated device that is tiny and easily hidden. It heats a flavored liquid until it vaporizes. The vapor is then inhaled into the user's lungs and blown out like smoke. Clouds of vapor from e-cigarettes are much less toxic than cigarette smoke to those in the vicinity—and also less offensive. There's no fire, ash, or unpleasant odor. Healthwise, the lure of vaping is simple. It promises to deliver nicotine's kick but without the dangers of lung cancer and other health problems that go along with a smoking habit. As a result lots of young people are regularly vaping at home, at school, or with friends.

Vaping products are not supposed to be sold or marketed to underage users. All fifty states have age restrictions on purchasing e-cigarettes. To buy e-cigs legally, a person must be at least eighteen years old with a valid photo ID. However, prior to a recent federal crackdown, such laws were not enforced uniformly. Teens would share information on which local convenience stores and vape shops were willing to sell e-cigs to minors. Younger teens also were able to obtain vaping products from older friends. Bans on underage use were largely ineffective.

Controversy has dogged e-cigarettes since they were introduced in the United States in 2006. The nicotine found in almost all types of e-liquids is highly addictive, just like the nicotine in tobacco cigarettes. Early reports that vaping is a safe alternative to traditional smoking have been tempered by more recent research. Studies show that long-term use of e-cigarettes exposes users to as much nicotine as smoking ordinary cigarettes. And more and more young people are becoming hooked on vaping. "It's impossible to let go once you started using," says Julien Lavandier, who began vaping as a high school sophomore. "I'll tell you—after even an hour and a half or two, I am chomping at the bit to find my Juul."[2]

"It's impossible to let go once you started using [an e-cigarette]. I'll tell you—after even an hour and a half or two, I am chomping at the bit to find my Juul."[2]

—Julien Lavandier, who began vaping as a high school sophomore

More studies are needed, but for now scientists warn that vaping may carry many of its own health consequences. These include lung disease, heart disease, and cancer. Chemicals in e-liquids may also pose a threat. Health risks are a particular concern for young users, whose brain development can be affected by the nicotine in e-cigarettes. Although not as dangerous as smoking ordinary cigarettes, it's clear that vaping is far from a risk-free pastime.

Widespread Use

Use of e-cigarettes continues to grow in the United States. International news site Reuters Health estimates that nearly one in twenty American adults are vaping regularly. More than half of these users are younger than age thirty-five. According to the *Annals of Internal Medicine*, about one-third of e-cigarette users vape every day.

The increase in vaping among teenagers has been even more dramatic. The National Youth Tobacco Survey reports that in 2018 more than 20 percent of high school students used e-cigarettes, an increase of 78 percent over the previous year. Even usage among middle school students showed an increase of 48 percent. Overall more teenagers today are vaping than are smoking cigarettes.

Because nicotine is so addictive, those who smoke tobacco cigarettes have a tough time quitting. Many smokers turn to vaping as a way to wean themselves off tobacco. However, studies show that using e-cigarettes rarely helps in kicking the tobacco habit. Health experts are more concerned about how vaping among teenagers can be a gateway to smoking traditional cigarettes. According to research, using e-cigarettes makes a person four times more likely to take up smoking tobacco than someone who does not vape.

A Push for Regulation

From school administrators to government health officials, there is concern that vaping is an epidemic that needs to be controlled. Critics claim that e-cigarette companies market their products to underage users. They point to e-liquid flavors such as gummy bear and cotton candy that seem obviously aimed at kids. Certain e-liquids are packaged to look like dessert toppings, cookies, and other food items. Vaping products are also sold online with what

Teen E-Cigarette Use Is Rapidly Growing

A national survey has revealed that 1.5 million more students in the United States used e-cigarettes in 2018 than in 2017. The increase among high school students during that one-year period was 78 percent, resulting in a total of 20.8 percent of high school students. The increase among middle school students was 48 percent, resulting in a total of 4.9 percent of middle school students. Public health officials and others say they are alarmed by the huge increase in e-cigarette use among US teenagers.

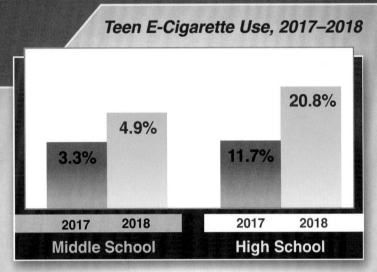

Teen E-Cigarette Use, 2017–2018

Source: US Food and Drug Administration, "Youth Tobacco Use: Results from the National Youth Tobacco Survey," November 2018. www.fda.gov.

critics say are insufficient safeguards against underage purchases. As a result, more cities and states are taking steps to regulate sales and usage of e-cigarettes. And some e-cigarette companies have responded to critics by changing their marketing pitch to focus on older users.

Despite the criticism, vaping retains its edgy allure among young people. E-cigarette companies use social media and online ads to stress the cool factor and downplay the negatives. The meteoric success of Juuls shows that the vaping trend still has plenty of juice in the marketplace. In vaping bars, at parties, and even in school restrooms, teens are blowing vapor clouds in ever-growing numbers.

CHAPTER ONE

The Basics of E-Cigarettes and Vaping

Vaping began as a way to help people stop smoking tobacco cigarettes. The idea was to provide nicotine without the harmful tar, carbon monoxide, and other substances associated with burning tobacco. In 1963 American inventor Herbert A. Gilbert obtained the first patent for a nontobacco cigarette. The modern version of the e-cigarette appeared forty years later. It was invented by Hon Lik, a pharmacist from Shenyang in northeast China. A heavy smoker himself, Hon was seeking a means to quit the habit, which had caused his father's fatal lung cancer. He tried various Chinese remedies as well as doses of nicotine to wean himself off cigarettes. One night before bed, Hon forgot to remove the nicotine patch he wore on his stomach to satisfy his smoker's craving. Hours later he awoke from bad dreams. He had dreamed that he was drowning until suddenly the water turned to vapor and he could breathe again. Inspired, Hon set about turning his dream into reality.

An Alternative to Cigarettes

Hon decided that the steady release of nicotine via the patch was inadequate. Heavy smokers like himself needed more intense nicotine highs to allow them to relax. Using his knowledge of mechanics and electronics, he created a device that looked like a cigarette and could heat a nicotine-laced liquid into vapor for inhaling. Hon obtained patents for his vaporizer in the United

States, enabling it to be sold worldwide. In China the device was called Ruyan, meaning "like smoke." At the time Hon could barely imagine how successful his invention would be.

His breakthrough created a huge new market for e-cigarettes and their liquids. In 2007 e-cigarettes began to appear in the United States at convenience stores, smoke shops, and mall kiosks. Internet campaigns promoted the new devices as an anti-smoking aid—sort of a halfway house on the road to quitting tobacco. Many longtime smokers turned to vaping as a healthier alternative to cigarettes, just as Hon intended. Early e-cigarette companies stressed the health aspects as well. "They are electronic, alternative smoking devices that simulate the sensation of smoking," says Craig Youngblood, president of e-cigarette maker InLife. "They do not expose

Hon Lik, who designed a modern version of the e-cigarette, demonstrates the use of his invention.

the user, or others close by, to harmful levels of cancer-causing agents and other dangerous chemicals normally associated with traditional tobacco products."[3]

In 2013 Hon sold his e-cigarette company for $75 million—although Hon himself received only a fraction of this amount. Ironically, Fontem Ventures, which snared the rights to Hon's invention, is part of Imperial Tobacco Group, one of the UK's largest tobacco firms. Today Hon travels the world for Fontem, which makes Blu e-cigs. He spreads the word about vaping and warns about the dangers of tobacco. Above all, Hon wants to be remembered for his efforts to curb smoking. It does not bother him that his employer is owned by a tobacco company. "What Fontem is doing is quite the opposite [from Imperial Tobacco]. Fontem shares my values," asserts Hon. "The e-cigarette is the alternative to smoking cigarettes."[4]

> "[E-cigarettes] are electronic, alternative smoking devices that simulate the sensation of smoking."[3]
>
> —Craig Youngblood, president of e-cigarette maker InLife

The Cloud Chasers

As the market for e-cigarettes grew, some companies began to experiment with new styles of vaporizers and new flavors for e-liquids. Some e-cigarettes looked like ordinary cigarettes with filters, while others resembled pens or markers. Designs became more efficient, and the number of choices available in e-liquids grew rapidly. A whole culture of young users sprang up to embrace the e-cigarette as a cool product in its own right. Pax Labs's 2015 introduction of Juuls, with their hip flash-drive design and trademark pods containing an extra jolt of nicotine, helped cement the youth craze for vaping. Juul offered pods with flavors aimed at attracting young users, such as mango, grape, and crème brûlée. Other brands, like Blu, Logic, and Njoy, also helped expand the youth market for e-cigarettes. Online forums gave teens a new platform in which to rate e-cigs and discuss the finer points of vaping. Overall more than 2 million middle and high school students today vape regularly. This growing legion of teenage vapers has made e-cigs into a cutting-edge lifestyle choice and a multibillion-dollar industry.

This development turned Hon Lik's original plan for e-cigs on its head. Health officials now worry that e-cigs will lead nonsmoking youths to try cigarettes. That is why, they contend, a huge tobacco firm like Altria Group is investing billions—$12.8 billion, to be exact—in the maker of Juuls. Although Juul Labs still claims its mission is to eliminate cigarettes, its marketing of ultrastylish e-cigarettes holds an obvious appeal for young people. "Juul says

The E-Cigarette That Mimics the Real Thing

For smokers looking to quit by switching to e-cigarettes, the cigalike (short for *cigarette-like*) is a popular choice. Cigalikes are small, light, and made to look like ordinary cigarettes. Their tan filter patterns have a familiar look for smokers. The LED tip that lights up fiery red when the user inhales helps mimic the process of smoking. Holding a lightweight cigalike feels natural to a smoker. This is important for a habit that is so wrapped up in ritual and repetitive movements. Smokers can occupy their hands and fill their lungs while experiencing much less harm from the many chemicals associated with smoke from burning tobacco.

When e-cigarettes first hit the American market, most of the devices were cigalikes. They heated e-liquid into mist via a mechanism that created ultrasonic vibrations. Most featured disposable plastic cartridges with saturated sponges inside. These early cigalikes produced much less vapor than today's e-cigs, and the sponges were less reliable than later cartridges. The technology of ultrasonic vibrations soon gave way to more efficient heating coils for a greater volume of vapor. Even today, cigalikes' small size presents shortcomings. The low-capacity battery necessary to fit in the small tube must be recharged more frequently than larger pod and box models. Heavy vapers must refill them with e-liquid much more often than with larger devices. Nonetheless, for as little as five dollars, a smoker can try a cigalike and embark on a path to potentially stop lighting up for good.

their goal is to save the lives of a billion smokers," says Robert Jackler, a Stanford physician who leads a team that researches the effects of tobacco advertising on youths. "You have to ask yourself, 'Is the company's behavior aligned with that goal?' I would have to say, sadly, no. . . . Their marketing in the first six months was patently youth-oriented."[5]

Hon dismisses all those enthusiastic young vapers as "cloud chasers." This refers to the popular stunt of cloud-chasing, or competing to blow the most enormous clouds of vapor from e-cigarettes. Hon hopes the youth-based fad for vaping itself will dissipate like a vapor cloud. He likens the cloud chasers to reckless hot-rodders. "When automotive manufacturers first started out, they were not thinking about a sport to be called Formula One," he says, referring to the car-racing competition. "You always have groups of people who are looking for excitement."[6]

"Juul says their goal is to save the lives of a billion smokers. You have to ask yourself, 'Is the company's behavior aligned with that goal?' I would have to say, sadly, no."[5]

—Robert Jackler, a Stanford physician who researches the effects of tobacco advertising on young people

How Vaping Works

Many young people are drawn to the sleek, cutting-edge aspect of e-cigarettes. They see them as smart cigarettes, without the ash, toxicity, and odor of smoking. The technology is simple and effective, with no match or fire involved. An e-cigarette consists of three parts: a rechargeable lithium battery, an atomizer tube with electronic controls, and a cartridge filled with e-liquid. The tip of the cartridge serves as a mouthpiece for inhaling. Inside the atomizer is a cotton and fiberglass wick. The wick is soaked in the e-solution, which is made of propylene glycol, vegetable glycerin, flavor aromas, and varying levels of nicotine. When the user pushes a button on the battery, heating coils wrapped around the wick heat the solution. This releases a vapor that mixes with the air. The user inhales the vapor through the mouthpiece, delivering nicotine to the lungs. The vapor is then exhaled in a cloud that quickly dissipates.

Some e-cigs, like the Juul, are mouth-activated and do not have a button to press before inhaling. To vape with a Juul, the user pops in an e-liquid pod and begins inhaling through the mouthpiece. The Juul device employs haptic feedback— electronic communication via the user's touch—to tell itself it is in use and to activate the heating element. It also turns itself off when not in use. This is the kind of smart technology kids have grown used to on their cell phones and other devices. In fact the lithium battery on a Juul can be recharged by plugging the device into the USB port on a laptop.

The battery for most vaping devices is permanently enclosed inside a casing. However, mods (short for modifieds) feature a battery that can be removed for recharging. This allows vapers to replace a run-down battery with one that is fully charged and ready. Mods tend to be thicker and heavier than standard e-cigarettes. They are prized by cloud chasers who seek longer vaping sessions.

Some e-cigs, like cigalikes, are built to mimic ordinary cigarettes. They have mouthpieces shaded like filters and red LED

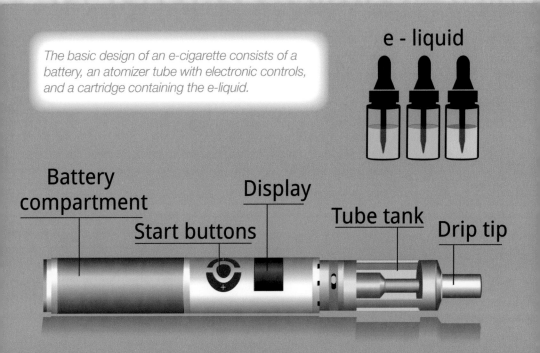

The basic design of an e-cigarette consists of a battery, an atomizer tube with electronic controls, and a cartridge containing the e-liquid.

e - liquid

Battery compartment

Display

Start buttons

Tube tank

Drip tip

lights on their ends that glow red as the user inhales. Former smokers often prefer cigalikes for the way they feel in their fingers and their overall similarity to cigarettes. They may also choose e-liquids that taste the most like ordinary cigarette smoke.

The Lowdown on E-Liquids

With the explosion in vaping sales, the number of e-liquids available has also soared. Like e-cigs, e-liquids go by many names, such as e-juice, pods, cartridges, or oil. Most e-liquids contain propylene glycol and/or vegetable glycerin. These are food additives approved for use by the US Food and Drug Administration (FDA),

Vaping Drugs in Plain Sight

Vaping is considered no big deal in some public places. But today some are using e-cigs to get high on illicit drugs, and they are doing it in public. Liquid forms of drugs can replace nicotine-based e-liquids for a sizeable but discreet high. Since e-cigs emit no smoke and little odor, it becomes difficult to perceive when an illegal substance is in use. Observers from parents and teachers to police officers may be fooled into thinking it is just another case of vaping. Meanwhile, the user may be vaping liquid THC, hash oil, synthetic marijuana, psychedelics, or some new and exotic substance suggested by friends. According to Sheriff's Lieutenant Ozzy Tianga of Broward County, Florida, "These individuals can smoke it right in front of you. And many times these vapes have no scent, or because they are a chemical substance the scent can be changed. It could be a fruit smell. It could be no smell at all."

Getting high this way presents a particular danger to young people. The vapor inhaled from e-cigs is absorbed into the user's bloodstream quickly through tiny air sacs in the lungs. This delivers an intense high that is extremely hazardous. Already the number of emergency room visits from those who vape with dangerous drugs is on the rise.

Quoted in Melissa Riddle Chalos, "Smoke and Mirrors: Does Vaping Make It Easy to Hide Drug Use?," *Michael's House Blog*. www.michaelshouse.com.

but they are not without drawbacks. Such chemicals are also employed in fog machines to create smoke effects at rock concerts. Concentrated exposure to them can cause lung irritation.

Those who vape have a choice of cartridges with different levels of nicotine—or none at all. The strength of e-liquids is usually measured in milligrams (weight) per milliliter (volume), or mg/mL. A typical range of concentrations is 3, 6, 12, and 18 mg/mL. By contrast, each puff from a Juul pod offers much more nicotine than most other e-liquids. Although a variety of strengths are available, many of the Juul pods run as high as 59 mg/mL. Juul's marketers also claim that its formulation of nicotine salts—a mixture of freebase nicotine and acids, including benzoic acid—helps increase the rate and amount of nicotine it delivers into the user's bloodstream.

Health experts say the amount of nicotine in e-liquids may vary wildly from the amount posted on the products' labels. A 2016 study at North Dakota State University looked at ninety-three e-cigarette liquids bought at sixteen stores in North Dakota. Researchers found that 51 percent of the e-liquids had nicotine levels different from that shown on the label. Of the mislabeled e-liquids, 17 percent had more nicotine than the labeled amount, and 34 percent had less. Some e-liquids were dangerously mislabeled, with nicotine amounts ranging from 66 percent less than the labeled amount to 172 percent more than the amount on the label. Even more troubling was the finding that some brands of e-liquids contained nicotine despite labels that claimed they were nicotine-free. According to Kelly Buettner-Schmidt, the study's author, levels of nicotine in e-liquids are a crucial consideration, particularly for young people. "Mislabeling of nicotine in e-liquids exposes the user to the harmful effects of nicotine," says Buettner-Schmidt. "In areas without child-resistant packaging requirements, children may be exposed to harmful nicotine."[7]

"Mislabeling of nicotine in e-liquids exposes the user to the harmful effects of nicotine."[7]

—Kelly Buettner-Schmidt, author of a 2016 study on e-liquids at North Dakota State University

Companies also tout the variety of flavors available for their e-cigarettes. E-liquid flavorings fall into five basic categories: fruit, drink, candy, dessert, and menthol. There are also tobacco flavorings for smokers who want something closer to the taste of smoking. Often the flavors combine categories, as with blueberry lemonade or raspberry cotton candy. Many people think these flavors, with their colorful names, are chosen strictly for their appeal to young users. Colorado congresswoman Diana DeGette introduced a bill to ban e-cigarette flavors nationally. "To me, there is no legitimate reason to sell any product with names such as cotton candy or tutti-frutti, unless you are trying to market it to children," asserts DeGette. "Most experts agree that the kid-friendly flavors that e-cigarette manufacturers are selling with these products are one of the leading causes of this spike in use among our high school and middle school students."[8]

How Teens Get Into E-Cigs

The variety of flavors is an important lure for young people who try e-cigarettes. The 2016 National Youth Tobacco Survey found that 31 percent of students who vaped were drawn to the availability of flavors. But the most common reason for trying e-cigs—mentioned by 39 percent in the survey—was because a friend or family member already was a user. Seventeen percent said they believed vaping was less harmful than other ways of using nicotine, including smoking cigarettes. Smaller percentages mentioned that e-cigs cost less than the tobacco variety or were easier to obtain.

All fifty states ban sales of e-cigarettes and vaping products to minors. Most state regulations on e-cigs are lumped in with the state's smoking laws. In addition the FDA continues to work on nationwide rules to control the sale and use of e-cigarettes. In 2018 the FDA began to require the following warning on all e-cigarettes sold in the United States: "WARNING: This product contains nicotine. Nicotine is an addictive chemical." Former FDA commissioner Scott Gottlieb has called youth vaping an epidemic. Gottlieb put e-cig manufacturers on notice that if they did not come up with plans to help prevent youth vaping, his agency would consider banning sales of their products. "Teenagers are becoming regular users, and the proportion of regular users is increasing," says Gottlieb. "We're going to have to take action."[9]

Despite these steps, high schoolers and middle schoolers continue to get their hands on vaping paraphernalia. Many get e-cigs from older students, friends, or siblings. They may be introduced to vaping at concerts or casual parties. Some are able to obtain e-cigs online at sites that lack filters for underage purchasers. These days the prize setup is the Juul "pod mod" device, which teens consider much hipper than standard e-cigarettes. According to Suchitra Krishnan-Sarin, coleader of the Yale Tobacco Center of Regulatory Science, "When we ask teens about their vaping or e-cig habits, they don't even consider juuling to be part of that."[10] And when they are partaking of outlandish e-juice flavors such as unicorn puke (a fruity mix like sherbet), the health consequences may not seem so serious.

A Costly Habit

Vaping generally is cheaper than smoking cigarettes, but it is still a costly habit. To begin, the user must buy a starter kit, including the e-cig device itself, a vaporizer, an atomizer or heating coil, e-liquid, and a charger. The cheapest kits cost less than $30, deliver about three hundred to four hundred puffs per charge, and last six months to a year if used with care. A basic Juul starter kit, with e-cig, USB charger, and four flavor pods, runs $50. Larger kits cost about $150 and allow for a thousand puffs per charge. Buying one vial of e-liquid every three to four weeks for moderate vaping costs from $15 to $30. Shelling out for the more intense kick of nicotine salts is even more expensive at $40 a vial. Atomizers get clogged and must be replaced at least every month or two, at a price of $1 to $6. Should the mod or battery break down, a replacement costs another $50 to $100. In general the monthly expense of vaping daily with premium liquids is about $40. For a former pack-a-day cigarette smoker, that can mean savings of about $160 per month. However, for a teenager with no history of tobacco use, vaping remains a considerable expense, with its own harmful effects to consider.

A Way to Quit Smoking?

Debates continue to rage about how effective e-cigs are in weaning smokers off tobacco cigarettes. To date, the FDA has not approved the use of e-cigarettes as a means to quit smoking. Nonetheless, vaping companies—including Hon Lik's employer—continue to promote e-cigs mainly as anti-smoking devices. Many former smokers swear by e-cigarettes and offer emotional testimony to their effectiveness. According to one former smoker: "The flavor alone [in e-cigarettes] was the key factor in helping me quit. It made it much more appealing to stick with it. . . . If it wasn't for vaping, I would have died from smoking cigarettes. Vaping has given me the opportunity to live longer and enjoy my children."[11]

"If it wasn't for vaping, I would have died from smoking cigarettes. Vaping has given me the opportunity to live longer and enjoy my children."[11]

—a former smoker who switched to e-cigarettes

Although health experts agree that vaping is less harmful than smoking tobacco, most studies have found that using e-cigarettes does not reduce smoking to a significant degree. Several studies have in fact shown the opposite—that vaping makes it more difficult to quit smoking. By using e-cigs, a person prolongs the addiction to nicotine. Moreover, vaping mimics the behaviors, gestures, and environmental cues linked to smoking tobacco, which often leads smokers back to cigarettes. Despite Hon Lik's hopes for his invention as a cure for smoking, experts remain skeptical. According to Linda Richter, director of Policy Research and Analysis for the Center on Addiction, "Given the limited evidence showing that e-cigarettes are an effective smoking cessation [quitting] aid and the growing body of evidence regarding their risks, the safest approach is to talk to your doctor about proven and effective cessation techniques."[12]

CHAPTER TWO

What Teens Are Saying About Vaping

Occasionally some teens from Atherton High School in Louisville, Kentucky, will gather for a party with a relaxed vibe. Friends are playing the video game *Fortnite*, watching YouTube, and taking hits from their e-cigs. Most of them vape casually, while others are hooked on the practice. Juuls are the preferred mode of vaping, considered to be the coolest choice, the Apple of e-cigarettes. Some also use Blu-brand devices shaped like portable battery packs. One girl describes a party trick where someone supposedly inhaled an entire Juul pod in a couple of epic hits. Another teen tries to re-create a trick he saw on YouTube by blowing massive smoke rings.

E-Cigs Are Easy to Score

To these teens, vaping is no big deal. Juuling is so rampant at school—in classrooms, in the cafeteria, in restrooms, in the parking lot—that it gets its own memes on Instagram. In one post a student joked about being surprised to find toilets in the Juul room. Most kids are focused more on how to score age-restricted e-liquids than with the health hazards associated with the practice. Some manage to purchase Juul pods at stores in town by acting calm and confident even though they are underage. The FDA recently cited eight local retailers for selling e-cigs to minors. The vape shops along Bardstown Road always check IDs, but kids in Louisville agree that it is not hard to get their hands on e-cigs. Many will pay a premium if siblings or older classmates will score vapes for them. "It's the same if you're, like, a drug dealer," says one student from duPont Manual High. "A Juul costs $50, so your fee is $80."[13]

Some teens make lots of money dealing e-cigs. They use pre-paid debit cards and a bit of guile to buy Juuls in bulk on websites like eBay and Alibaba. Some sell pods at school, some sell full devices, some offer exotic flavors of e-liquids for refills. According to Leslie, a sixteen-year-old girl in Westchester County, New York, teens at her school start juuling at parties to relax. Then they end up buying the devices from classmates, recharging their Juuls on

Many teens consider vaping to be no big deal, and the practice is rampant at schools.

laptops, and posting videos of themselves vaping on Snapchat and Instagram. Leslie says dealing Juuls is a regular business:

> Dealers will announce on Snapchat that they've bought a hundred of them, and they'll write the price, the date, and the meeting place for kids to show up with cash. . . . The biggest spots are the bathrooms. There are so many people Juuling sometimes that all the varieties of flavors just get morphed into one big vape. Some days I'm just, like, why do you need to do this at 11 a.m.?[14]

Leslie notes that many kids vape to relieve their anxiety, but they do not want to let it show: "You're expected to Juul, but you're expected to not depend on it. If you're cool, then you Juul with other people, and you post about it, so everyone will see that you're social and ironic and funny. But, if you're addicted, you go off by yourself and Juul because you need it, and everyone knows."[15]

Leslie also views e-cigs as exclusively the property of teenagers like herself. She says she is always surprised to see an adult juuling, which to her is like her grandmother using Alexa, Amazon's robot assistant.

"You're expected to Juul, but you're expected to not depend on it. . . . If you're addicted, you go off by yourself and Juul because you need it, and everyone knows."[15]

—Leslie, a sixteen-year-old in Westchester County, New York

A Disturbing Epidemic

Dante Caloia also connects vaping with his own generation. The high school senior sees it going on every day at his school in Ottawa, the capital of Canada in southern Ontario. Caloia thinks that e-cigs are becoming an epidemic capable of damaging young lives. He points out that lots of teens are taken in by vaping stunts on YouTube and other social media, such as blowing enormous smoke rings or exhaling mini-tornadoes. He doubts these kids recognize the dangers:

When I go to school, I see kids as young as Grade 9 skipping class or going into the bathroom to take a hit from a vape. My worry is that this creates an addiction. I know several people my age who can't go a few minutes without shaking and craving their vapes. They say it's harmless, but I don't think it is.

The fact that kids are doing this at school is another problem. I have often walked into the bathroom and seen kids huddled in a circle passing their vapes around. Sometimes I come in and my eyes instantly hurt from the clouds of nicotine and chemicals that are left in the air. . . .

Just today I saw something so disturbing, I decided to do something. I saw a boy in Grade 10 walking in front of me to use the washroom, I assumed. He then proceeded to double over and throw up all over the wall and the floor. He then staggered to the stall and vomited all over it as well. I have seen other students vomit in garbage cans, too.

Pediatricians have warned about vaping and liquid nicotine overdose, which can cause vomiting. Kids at school call this "nicking out."[16]

Caloia believes parents and adults have yet to realize the magnitude of the epidemic that vaping has become. School bans have had little effect on student vaping, he says, and more needs to be done to stop the practice. He admits he once tried vaping at a party. Although he didn't like it, he could understand how some kids might be attracted.

The administration at Caloia's school has started an anti-vaping committee based on some of his suggestions. He hopes the committee will spread the word that many students and teachers have had it with the vaping craze. Caloia thinks that learning about the risks of nicotine could discourage students from vaping—especially if the message comes not from teachers or parents but from their own classmates.

Some teens have tried to persuade their peers to not use e-cigarettes. Utah teens (pictured) rally for a higher tax on the devices in order to discourage their use.

Other students at Caloia's West Carleton High School do not have a problem with vaping. They see it as a practical alternative to the craving for cigarettes. As one student explains: "I vape because it gets the cravings away. It's not the same as a cigarette because you don't really feel it going down your throat. You still get a buzz, but it's not exactly the same. I'd say it's a lot healthier because it cuts down a lot of the toxic chemicals and all the stuff that's from actually burning."[17]

An Addictive Fad

Some young people are already becoming jaded about the vaping fad. They started in order to avoid cigarettes at parties and then became addicted to the nicotine hits. John and Zoe are teens in

New York who make fun of the e-cig hype, which they say blew up for two years and now barely interests them:

John: You'd go into a bathroom and everyone would be ripping them. A few months ago people would do it in the library too. If you rip it and hold it in, you can't see it, smell it, nothing. It's pretty funny. Now it's less, though, because the school found out, so people do it in their cars.

Zoe: That year it had a certain cachet and I felt cool that I had one. And then in the middle of tenth grade, it changed. It wasn't not cool but it was just another thing in my life that I was using and I didn't think of the connotation anymore. None of us smoked before we Juuled. At some point we started it 'cause we thought it was cool and then we kept using it 'cause we got addicted.

John: It's a stigma these days that kids don't want to be associated with cigarettes. Most of the kids who started actually used it instead of cigarettes. That was me. If I was at a party and I didn't want to smoke I would rip the Juul outside. A few people started with it and then other kids saw it at parties and then it became cool. . . .

Zoe: Usually things that were fads would've phased out already. I do think it's notable that it's been around for longer than things that are a fad normally are. And a reason is that [it] does cause nicotine addictions and the people using them are addicted to nicotine, so that's going [to] keep them around.

John: Honestly, I'm trying to quit and I know a lot of kids who are quitting. Especially the kids who weren't into it and just bought it to be cool. Any addiction isn't good. People are using it all the time, most of them weren't smoking before, which is the funny thing. Most kids these days use it because they saw their friends using it. . . .

Zoe: Now there are three camps: you use Juul and like it. You formerly used a Juul and realized it probably wasn't great. Or you don't get the hype around it. . . . I threw out my Juul mid-January and it became so clear to me in that moment how uncool it was. Now I think everyone who does it is so dumb but there were two years that I thought it was so cool. I look at someone with a Juul and remember how carefree I was.[18]

"Love at First Puff"

Matt Murphy figures he is pretty much a typical high school vaper in the way he got hooked. At age sixteen, he went to a party in a friend's basement in Reading, Massachusetts, with kids swigging vodka from water bottles, chasing it with Diet Coke, and shouting back and forth over deafening hip-hop. There he tried his first Juul. He liked the minty flavor in his mouth, but when he inhaled the vapor to the back of his throat and deep into his lungs, the force of the nicotine "head rush," as he calls it, was like nothing he had ever experienced. "It was love at first puff," he recalls.[19]

Chasing that euphoric feeling, Murphy kept asking his friends for another hit of their Juuls. Soon he was juuling so often he referred to the little device as his eleventh finger. He hated his growing dependency, but time and again that intense rush proved irresistible. On the third vape-less day of a family vacation, Murphy broke down and Ubered to a local shop, where he laid down money for a starter kit. His juuling habit of one or more pods a day soon was costing him forty dollars a week. He and his athlete buddies kept vaping even though their shortness of breath was obvious. "We called it 'Juul lung,'" says

"You'd go into a bathroom and everyone would be ripping [e-cigs]. A few months ago people would do it in the library too. If you rip it and hold it in, you can't see it, smell it, nothing. It's pretty funny."[18]

—John, a high school student in New York City

Restroom Surveillance for Vapers

Teens who vape at school like to refer to the restroom as the Juul room. However, it is no joke for school officials trying to keep students from using e-cigs. Schools have resorted to several unsatisfactory methods to discourage vaping, such as removing stall doors and posting bathroom monitors. Now many schools are installing surveillance systems in restrooms to catch vapers in the act. More than two hundred schools across the United States and Canada are employing Fly Sense, a system powered by artificial intelligence or AI. Although schools cannot legally place cameras in their restrooms, Fly Sense uses other types of sensors to detect the chemical traces of vapors from Juuls and other e-cigarettes. The system sends real-time alerts by text or e-mail to school officials.

Soter Technologies, the maker of Fly Sense, reports that the system's accuracy rate for detecting vaping runs between 70 percent and 80 percent. Despite the fairly high number of false alarms, the company states that the mere presence of Fly Sense in school restrooms acts as a deterrent to the use of e-cigs. "Schools typically install the system and see a spike of vaping incidents in the first two weeks," says Derek Peterson, CEO of Soter Technologies. "And then as they continue to go through their school policy plan of reprimanding the students, they start to see vaping incidents in those locations trail off." Fly Sense and other sensor systems might be the best compromise between privacy and detection to deter student vaping.

Quoted in Jeremy Hsu, "Schools Enlist AI to Detect Vaping and Bullies in Bathrooms," *IEEE Spectrum*, October 30, 2018. www.spectrum.ieee.org.

Murphy. "We knew it lowered our performance but we saw that as a sacrifice we were willing to make." And he also grew to enjoy taking discreet puffs under the noses of his parents and teachers: "The Juul was super, super sneaky and I loved it."[20]

At college Murphy worked his e-cig habit into his daily routine. His craving for regular hits made him irritable if not satisfied. He kept a Juul attached to the wall over his dorm room bed so he could get his necessary rush as soon as he woke up. His friends noticed the disconnect between Murphy's vaping and his disdain for e-cigs. "Matt was open about wishing he didn't do it," says Tucker Houston, Murphy's freshman roommate.

"It was a constant battle for him. People would tell him that they'd want to buy a Juul and he'd be like, 'No! You don't want to, it's not cool, it's not fun.' He became known as the juuling anti-Juul advocate."[21]

On a construction job during the summer, Murphy would go several hours without vaping. Then, after work, he would indulge in "zeroing," one of his fa-

"People would tell [Matt] that they'd want to buy a Juul and he'd be like, 'No! You don't want to, it's not cool, it's not fun.' He became known as the juuling anti-Juul advocate."[21]

—Tucker Houston, Matt Murphy's freshman roommate

The addiction to the nicotine in e-cigarettes is powerful, and withdrawal symptoms can be unpleasant.

Vaping for Fun and Stress Relief on Campus

E-cigs are blowing up at colleges just like at high schools. Many users begin vaping on campus, joining a growing number of their friends who vape. Nineteen-year-old Cassandri Cini started juuling during her freshman year at the suggestion of her boyfriend at the time. She says her friends do not think of e-cigs as something tobacco-related and risky. "In college, a lot of people have them," she says. "When we go out people will share them. I think cigarettes are super gross, but vaping seems cleaner almost. You don't think of them like cigarettes." Once she got hooked, however, Cini found it hard to quit. She needs her Juul to avoid headaches and shaky nerves. "It's so stupid to say it out loud, but I literally just got addicted to it because it was a social thing," she says. "I've definitely tried to stop, but it's like an addiction, so you can't really stop."

Other college students, like nineteen-year-old Leia Dyste of Northern Arizona University, turn to e-cigs for stress relief instead of cigarettes. Dyste likes vaping because it carries fewer carcinogens than regular smoking. "The act itself of smoking is not a crutch, but something I rely on to ease anxiety, and vaping is an easy way to do that," says Dyste. "For those who do smoke cigarettes, or have in the past, it's like a healthier alternative even if we don't know everything about all the risks yet."

Quoted in Marina Pitofsky, "Millions of Teens Are Vaping Every Day. Here's What They Have to Say About the Growing Trend," *USA Today*, December 21, 2018. www.usatoday.com.

vorite routines. He would draw a huge Juul hit into his lungs and hold it until his body had absorbed all the vapor. Four or five of these super-hits left him dizzy but satisfied. For Murphy, the wait was worth it. "I knew if my parents caught me, I couldn't do it again, and that represented a future of not doing it," he admits. "I rationalized that it was better to do without it briefly, than forever. . . . If you wait an hour, it feels great. But if you wait five hours, it feels unbelievable."[22]

When his parents finally did discover his habit, there was an uncomfortable scene. Murphy decided to quit, but breaking free proved to be not so easy. He made a show of tossing his Juul out the window of a friend's car. However, his powerful addiction soon left him huddled in bed with a case of the shakes. The whirring sound of a friend's Juul powering up would trigger the worst cravings. Three hellish weeks finally passed and the cravings diminished. Now when Murphy is tempted to vape again, he reminds himself of all that he went through. He constantly hears from friends who are thinking about quitting. "They text me all the time when they're trying," says Murphy. "They'll say, 'Did you experience this?' And I say, 'Yes,' because I want them to know I understand. And then I tell them, 'But it gets better.' Because it does."[23] Murphy still keeps track of the days since his last hit of an e-cigarette.

CHAPTER THREE

What Is Everyone Worried About?

Sarah, a mother of two living in Ann Arbor, Michigan, was stunned when the principal at her son's middle school called to say he'd been suspended. A parent had taken photos of Sarah's son and another boy vaping on school grounds after class. At first Sarah thought the principal was overreacting. She did not know much about vaping, but she knew her son, a straight A student, had always been responsible and trustworthy. A brief talk with the principal opened her eyes, how-ever. Sarah learned that the principal had almost called the police. "The principal knows that vaping is common and shared that the businesses in down-town Ann Arbor are selling to teens without asking for IDs," says Sarah. "However, she feels the need to let my son and his friends know that it's a really, really big deal."[24]

> "The principal knows that vaping is common. . . . However, she feels the need to let my son and his friends know that it's a really, really big deal."[24]
>
> —Sarah, a mother of two living in Ann Arbor, Michigan

Knowing the Facts

Health professionals stress the importance of knowing the facts about vaping and e-cigs. According to Sarper Taskiran, a child and adolescent psychiatrist at the Child Mind Institute, too many teenagers view e-cigs as a harmless fad. "They really think that they are mostly flavors," he notes, "and that they are inhaling

a pleasant gas."[25] For many young people, smoking retains an aura of cool in movies and videos, and vaping can seem like an even cooler approach. Warnings about the risks and drawbacks connected with vaping may strike teens as needless alarm. With this in mind, Taskiran urges parents to engage their kids in a talk about e-cigarettes. Parents might ask if lots of kids at school are vaping, for instance, and they could work up to questions about what vaping is like. Sarah's husband got their son to open up about his first experience with e-cigarettes even before the boy knew about the principal's call. "They had a full one hour conversation about it after I was already asleep," says Sarah. "He told my husband that he tried it for the first time and that it burned his throat and he didn't like it."[26] Taskiran contends that children, parents, and school officials should educate themselves about the vaping boom.

A Growing Youth Market

Vaping is often promoted as a healthier—or less harmful— alternative to smoking cigarettes. Manufacturers of e-cigs stress the product's function as an aid to quit smoking. However, under-age users, many of whom have never smoked, represent a grow-ing percentage of the market for e-cigarettes. A 2018 national survey conducted by the University of Michigan found that 30 percent of high school seniors, 25 percent of tenth graders, and 11 percent of eighth graders claimed to have vaped with nicotine in the past year.

The Truth Initiative, a nonprofit public health group opposed to tobacco use, joined with researchers from three universities for an-other survey of nine thousand minors and an additional four thou-sand younger adults about vaping. That study found that 6 percent of fifteen- to seventeen-year-olds and 8 percent of eighteen- to twenty-one-year-olds had vaped with a Juul from one to thirty times in the past month. The Centers for Disease Control and Prevention says these figures are about the same as for smoking standard cigarettes. By contrast, only about 1 percent of those aged twenty-five to thirty-four had vaped in the past month. Confronted with these numbers by the online news site Business Insider, a spokes-person for Juul responded that "underage use is directly opposed to our mission of eliminating combustible cigarettes by offering the world's one billion existing adult smokers a true alternative."[27]

Nevertheless, researchers see these figures as proof that e-cigarette use is growing rapidly among teens in the United States. In fact the data in the Truth Initiative survey may already be un-derstating the problem. As the researchers noted, "While rates of Juul use are highest among the younger segments of the sample, the data only reflects use patterns from February through May 2018. The most recent Nielsen sales data for Juul indicate dra-matic increases since then."[28]

In other words, e-cigs and vaping paraphernalia are flying off the shelves in vaping shops and online sources, and they are ending up in the hands of young people in increasing numbers. Some users are very young indeed. Sonya Kennedy, who owns a dance studio in Northern California, was stunned to learn that Ryder, her twelve-year-old son, was vaping. He and his friends were taking secretive puffs in class and even charging their e-cigs on their teacher's computer. "He honestly didn't think that there was anything wrong," Kennedy says. "He told me that almost all the grade-sevens were doing it."[29]

Addiction to Nicotine

The main hazard for young people who use e-cigarettes is becoming addicted to nicotine. Almost all pods and e-juices for e-cigs contain a certain amount of nicotine. The ostensible purpose is to provide cigarette smokers a less harmful method of getting their nicotine fix while weaning themselves off tobacco. Because e-cigs involve heating a liquid rather than burning tobacco, vaping is considered to be a smokeless alternative. Many smokers prefer it to chewing nicotine gum or wearing a nicotine patch. Moreover, vaping actually is less dangerous than smoking cigarettes. According to the American Cancer Society, lighting up a cigarette and inhaling the smoke exposes a person to an estimated seven thousand chemicals and toxins, more than ninety of which are linked to cancer and heart disease. Taking in nicotine without burning tobacco is a positive step for any smoker seeking to quit. Most smokers are already addicted to nicotine when they begin vaping, so inhaling this additive in e-liquids is not a large concern compared to the overall benefits of not lighting up.

For young people who vape, however, nicotine is a serious problem. Many begin using e-cigs with the idea that the water vapor filling their lungs is essentially harmless—just flavored mist. Instead, with each puff they are getting a strong dose of nicotine. Because of the nicotine, frequent vaping can be just as addictive as smoking. Research shows that individuals who begin vaping

Vaping and the Immune System

Scientists warn that vaping may damage the immune system, especially in vulnerable teens. In a recent study at Johns Hopkins Bloomberg School of Public Health, researchers found that mice subjected to vapor from e-cigarettes suffered from weaker immune systems than those breathing fresh air. After breathing e-cig vapor for two weeks in doses that mimicked regular use, the mice were exposed to microbes that caused an illness such as pneumonia. The mice subjected to vaping showed a weakened immune response, developing infections that were much more severe than those of the fresh-air control group. For some of the vaping mice, the infections proved lethal. "The e-cigarette exposure inhibited the ability of mice to clear the bacteria from their lungs," says lead author Thomas Sussan, "and the viral infection led to increased weight loss and death indicative of an impaired immune response."

Teenage vapers might dismiss studies on mice, but research on human cells at the University of North Carolina also leads to concern about vaping and the immune system. Researchers examined cells scraped from inside the noses of smokers and vapers who were otherwise healthy. They discovered that immune-system activity was reduced in 53 genes for both smokers and vapers. However, those who vaped saw immune-system activity depressed in another 305 genes. Apparently certain e-liquids can affect the ability of immune cells to fight infection. Smoking tobacco has long been identified as damaging to a person's immune system. Now it appears the same may be true of vaping.

Quoted in IFL Science!, "E-Cigarette Vapor Shown to Repress Immune System." www.iflscience.com.

can become addicted in a short time. Once hooked on nicotine, users find it hard to quit. In fact, the younger a person is, the more vulnerable he or she is to nicotine addiction and long-term cravings. "Everybody has a certain amount of nicotine receptors in the brain," says K. Vendrell Rankin, director of Tobacco Treatment Services at Texas A&M University. "When you start smoking, vaping or supplying nicotine to them, they multiply. If you stop smoking or vaping, the receptors don't go away."[30] When the receptors increase in number, teens require more nicotine to get the same high. That in turn leads them to take hit after hit from their e-cigs.

Experts say that Juuls are especially hazardous because their e-liquid pods offer a larger nicotine kick than competing brands.

Often this results in side effects, such as difficulty focusing and bouts of anxiety or depression.

The nicotine hazard is compounded with Juuls, the e-cigs of choice for a large percentage of young people who vape. E-liquid pods for Juuls tend to offer a larger nicotine kick than competitors' brands. This is because they are made from nicotine salts, like those found in loose-leaf tobacco, instead of the standard nicotine freebase used in most e-liquids. Nicotine salts increase the amount and rate of nicotine that enters the user's bloodstream. In the past Juul has promoted the speed with which its product delivers nicotine—up to 2.7 times faster than other e-cigs. One Juul pod provides about two hundred puffs, or the nicotine equivalent of a pack of cigarettes. Depending on how often a teenager vapes, he or she could be getting a potent—and addictive—dose of nicotine on a regular basis.

Risk to Brain Development

Young people who vape are also risking harm to their developing brains. The brain does not reach full development until about age twenty-five. Until then, various areas of the brain can be permanently affected by a substance like nicotine. Each puff from an e-cig sends nicotine to the brain within seven seconds. Adolescents who vape repeatedly with nicotine can damage parts of the brain dealing with learning, attention span, mood, and impulse control.

Young people's brains form synapses—or strong connections between brain cells—at a more rapid rate than adult brains. These synapses, which create memories and allow for learning, can be disrupted by nicotine use. Nicotine also unlocks receptor cells in the brain that provide a message of well-being or pleasure. This can produce feelings of calm satisfaction during vaping, a feel-good high. However, repeated exposure can cause brain cells to change. This can limit the brain's ability to release its natural chemicals for pleasure, such as dopamine. Some health experts worry that vaping during early adolescence could lead to a lifelong risk of addiction.

Nicotine addiction can also make quitting e-cigs an ordeal for young users. Some individuals who have stopped both smoking and vaping say the latter habit is harder to break. Once a person tries to quit vaping, feelings of fatigue take over for two or three days. Then the cravings for another puff intensify. The ability to concentrate dwindles, and headaches, nausea, and agitation usually follow. Many teens who have quit vaping say they would reach for their e-cigs every few minutes for weeks. Jonathan Winickoff, a pediatrician at Massachusetts General Hospital for Children, says most of his middle and high school patients find the nicotine withdrawal so difficult they simply stop trying to quit. "They have an inability to concentrate and a pervasive desire to use the substance," he states. "It overwhelms anything else the adolescent is doing. They become annoyed, anxious, and don't want to do anything but get the nicotine their brain needs."[31]

Scientific studies continue to emphasize the kind of damage nicotine can do to adolescent brains. "We have a lot of evidence showing that the adolescent brain is extremely sensitive to the effects of nicotine," says Suchitra Krishnan-Sarin, coleader of the Yale Tobacco Center of Regulatory Science. "Studies have shown us that nicotine can interfere with memory and attention processing."[32] Krishnan-Sarin believes it is urgent that young people learn about the damaging effects of nicotine from vaping.

A Gateway to Cigarettes

Cigarette smoking has declined among teenagers, and today more American teens vape than smoke. Yet health experts fear that nicotine addiction from vaping may lead teens to take up smoking tobacco, reversing Hon Lik's original purpose for inventing the e-cigarette. The National Institute on Drug Abuse reports that 30.7 percent of teens start smoking tobacco cigarettes within six months of vaping e-cigs. A 2017 study conducted by the University of Illinois Pediatrics Department found that teens who vape are seven times more likely to smoke cigarettes later than teens who do not. Researchers surveyed more than 1,400 high school students annually for three years running to isolate the trend.

In addition the study determined that the influence did not run both ways. In other words, teens who smoked tobacco cigarettes showed no increased like-

"[Withdrawal from nicotine] overwhelms anything else the adolescent is doing. They become annoyed, anxious, and don't want to do anything but get the nicotine their brain needs."[31]

—Jonathan Winickoff, a pediatrician at Massachusetts General Hospital for Children

"We have a lot of evidence showing that the adolescent brain is extremely sensitive to the effects of nicotine. Studies have shown us that nicotine can interfere with memory and attention processing."[32]

—Suchitra Krishnan-Sarin, coleader of the Yale Tobacco Center of Regulatory Science

lihood of switching to e-cigs. "The rising frequency of recent e-cigarette use among youth over time is concerning," the study's authors write, "especially in light of evidence that e-cigarette use is a significant risk factor for future conventional cigarette use."[33] The authors believe teens who become hooked on nicotine may turn to tobacco cigarettes in order to get a bigger kick for their money. Whatever the reason, the trend is worrisome for adolescents, who are more vulnerable to nicotine's ill effects. Moreover, developing a smoking habit can lead to lung cancer, heart disease, emphysema, and many other long-term health problems.

As e-cigs rocket upward in popularity, some teens are experimenting with vaping other substances, including marijuana.

Exploding E-Cigs

Smoking tobacco cigarettes is unquestionably more harmful than vaping. But at least standard cigarettes do not present a danger of exploding. There have been several incidents of e-cigs overheating and exploding in the United States and other countries. In 2018 a TV producer named Tallmadge D'Elia died at his Florida home when his vaping device blew up and pierced his skull with metal fragments. Others have suffered severe burns from vaping blasts. Cases in which e-cigs explode are rare, but teenage users should be aware of the dangers.

E-cigarettes contain a lithium-ion battery, which must be handled correctly to avoid safety issues. Problems arise usually when changing a battery. E-cigarettes generally have safety features to prevent dangerous heat buildup, but some users invite trouble by modifying their devices. According to Mark Gardiner, a product safety expert, "Enthusiasts might experiment with different batteries and e-liquids to try and get the biggest vape. This can result in people building their own systems which can generate a lot of heat and then explode." Gardiner admits, however, that any device with a lithium-ion battery has the capability of dangerously overheating. "And if a battery fails and explodes," he adds, "then obviously it's an extra hazard if it's in your mouth."

Quoted in Laurel Ives, "How Likely Is Your E-Cigarette to Explode?," BBC News, May 18, 2018. www.bbc.com.

Some teens are experimenting with vaping other substances, such as marijuana.

One survey suggests that as many as one in eleven US students have tried marijuana in e-cigarettes. In states where marijuana sales are legal, consumers can buy e-liquid cartridges that contain THC, the ingredient in pot that generates a high. Such products are not sold legally to minors, but teens often can get their hands on the latest e-juice of whatever kind. Health officials worry that the social environment linked to vaping—the drive to be hip and open to experiment—might increase the risk of drug use for young people.

Other Dangerous Chemicals
Nicotine is not the only harmful substance associated with vaping. For example, formaldehyde, a cancer-causing agent, can

form if e-liquid overheats or if less than enough liquid makes it to the heating element—a situation called a "dry puff." E-cigs and their vapor may also contain volatile organic compounds (VOCs). These toxins can damage a user's kidneys, liver, and nervous system. VOCs also cause eye, nose, and throat irritation, as well as headaches and nausea.

Many e-liquids, such as those with vanilla, maple, or coconut flavoring, contain the chemical diacetyl, a buttery-flavored additive found in popcorn and caramel. Diacetyl has been linked to bronchiolitis obliterans, a serious and nonreversible lung disease. This condition, also called popcorn lung, scars the lungs' tiny air sacs and leaves the airways thickened and narrowed. Popcorn lung causes a person to cough, wheeze, and experience shortness of breath, much like the symptoms of lung failure called chronic obstructive pulmonary disease or COPD. In light of these hazards, makers of candy and popcorn have removed diacetyl from their products, but manufacturers of e-liquids have yet to follow suit. Harvard researchers found that thirty-nine out of fifty-one e-cigarette brands include diacetyl. The American Lung Association has urged the FDA and other regulators to crack down on diacetyl and other harmful chemicals contained in e-liquids.

Teens Need to Be Informed

As e-cigarette use among teens continues to grow, health experts stress the importance of getting the truth out about vaping. Too many young people believe inhaling the flavored vapor from e-cigs is basically a harmless amusement. In reality the nicotine in e-liquids is highly addictive and can lead to a variety of health problems. Nicotine's effect on adolescents' developing brains is a particular concern. Efforts to quit e-cigs result in withdrawal symptoms that can leave teens feeling anxious or depressed. Studies also show that vaping often leads young people to begin smoking cigarettes, which is the opposite of e-cigarettes' supposed justification as an anti-smoking aid.

Overall, teens and their parents need more information about the effects of vaping. "We end up needing to teach kids how they can deal with cravings, how they can identify high-risk situations, how they can actually deal with being surrounded by people who are using [e-cigarettes]," says Dr. Sharon Levy, director of the Adolescent Substance Use and Addiction Program at Boston Children's Hospital. "Because the reality is that, for most kids, we treat them and put them back in school, and then they go to the bathroom, and everybody's Juuling."[34]

"We end up needing to teach kids how they can deal with cravings, how they can identify high-risk situations, how they can actually deal with being surrounded by people who are using [e-cigarettes]."[34]

—Dr. Sharon Levy, director of the Adolescent Substance Use and Addiction Program at Boston Children's Hospital

CHAPTER FOUR

Do E-Cigarette Companies Target Teens?

In August 2018 Sabrina Zampa discovered a Juul vaporizer in her son's bedroom at her home in Miami, Florida. When she confronted him, she was stunned to find out that both her teenage sons had been vaping since middle school. Her older boy, who was sixteen, told her he had purchased his first Juul on the company's website by lying about his age. For several years he and his brother, who is two years younger, had used an online delivery service called Postmates to get pod replacements because Postmates did not require ID or proof of age. Now Zampa fears both her sons are addicted to juuling. She says she had no idea that Juul contains nicotine or that it was developed to maximize the nicotine's narcotic effect. As a result of her discovery, on November 5, Zampa filed suit against Juul in the Miami-Dade Circuit Court. Her ultimate goal: to stop Juul and other e-cigarette companies from targeting children.

Marketing to Children

Zampa's lawsuit against Juul is part of a class action—a lawsuit filed by a small group acting on behalf of a larger affected group. Her complaint is joined by several parents across the nation. The suit claims the company knowingly marketed its products to children to get them hooked. As Zampa acknowledges, her sons spent hundreds of dollars on Juul flavor pods—especially their favorite, "cool cucumber"—to stoke their vaping habit. She insists neither of her sons were aware of the nicotine in Juuls or the threat of addiction. The suit declares that Zampa's sons, like the other class members, were lured by Juul's deceptive marketing efforts, which presented its products as safe and candy-like. It claims they suffered from exposure to nicotine at toxic levels without sufficient warning. Attempts to quit resulted in the boys getting headaches and nausea. They had to resume vaping just to avoid these ill effects.

Zampa's attorney, John Yanchunis, blames Juul's marketing approach for the teens' addiction. "Our interest is representing a class of children who have been enticed, induced, and attracted to these products," Yanchunis says. "Particularly for a young person, a child, it's much harder to overcome something that is

Some teens obtain their e-cigarettes through online delivery services (such as Postmates), which may not require ID or proof of age.

addictive than, say, an adult who may have more maturity and a greater strength of willpower. It's a significant problem."[35] For its part, Juul insists the lawsuit has no merit and promises to defend itself against all claims.

Barbara Yannucci, another Florida mother, is also suing Juul in federal court. Her fifteen-year-old son J.Y. got hooked on Juul e-cigs after seeing other kids in his high school vaping. He started buying Juul pods at his local Wawa convenience store. Addicted now, J.Y. vapes up to twelve times a day. Yannucci's suit cites Juul for fraud and negligence in its marketing blitz. According to Yannucci's attorney, the e-cig maker knew its nicotine-based products were more potent and addictive than advertised. In addition the company allegedly targeted underage users with an array of kid-friendly fruit and candy flavors.

The Appeal of Exotic Flavors

Offering exotic flavors to attract teenage users is hardly a new ploy in the tobacco industry. Controversy over flavored tobacco products goes back to 2009, when the US Congress banned flavors in tobacco cigarettes to discourage youth sales. The ban included cigarettes such as Camel's Twista Lime, Margarita Mixer, Warm Winter Toffee, Mocha Mint, and other fruit and candy flavors. However, the ban did not apply to e-cigarette flavors. Makers of e-cigs continued to market and sell all sorts of exotic-flavored e-juices with obvious appeal to teens. Just as with tobacco cigarettes, flavored e-liquids like gummy bear, cotton candy, peanut butter cup, Pop Rocks, and cookies and cream attract kids by reducing the harsh taste of vaping and making it easier to get hooked on e-cigs.

With this in mind, anti-smoking groups like the Campaign for Tobacco-Free Kids have urged the FDA to ban all flavored tobacco products without exception. But health experts warn that eliminating flavored e-cigs might deter longtime smokers from using them as a much less harmful alternative to tobacco. Supporting responsible adult usage while trying to dissuade kids from vaping can be a delicate balance. "I don't envy [the] FDA," says Kenneth Warner, professor emeritus of the University of Michigan School of Public Health. "Finding the 'sweet spot' of e-cigarette regulation is tough. Most anything they do to discourage youth vaping will risk reducing the usefulness of vaping as [a] smoking cessation aid."[36]

"Finding the 'sweet spot' of e-cigarette regulation is tough. Most anything they do to discourage youth vaping will risk reducing the usefulness of vaping as [a] smoking cessation aid."[36]

—Kenneth Warner, professor emeritus of the University of Michigan School of Public Health

E-cigarette companies avow that their main purpose is to help people stop smoking. And e-cig companies insist that marketing vapes to underage children is not only impractical, it is a poor business strategy: it invites more local and federal regulations on how they sell and market their products. As for the complaints about candy- and fruit-flavored e-liquids, industry spokespeople point out that sweet products sell to all demographics. As Gianna Delmonte, who has worked in the vaping industry since 2015, says:

> How is it deemed that children are the only age group consuming candy, fruit, and desserts? There is no age limit on enjoying sweets; and simply because you are an adult does not mean you will go after savory flavors such as tobacco over sweet ones based on your age. . . . Only the tiniest fraction of electronic cigarette and vaporizer companies are targeting kids. Otherwise, the rest of us, the 99%, are striving to maintain the integrity of this industry, and are interested in an adults-only customer base.[37]

A Natural Customer Base

Despite such protestations, the vaping industry continues to receive criticism for allegedly targeting teenagers and children in its ads and marketing. Some critics claim tobacco interests—many of which own e-cig companies—are trying to secure life-time customers by getting youths hooked on nicotine. Whatever their motives, from the beginning e-cig companies have focused on a hip, colorful brand that appeals to young people. Teenagers and children are exposed to marketing for e-cigarettes in various ways, helping to make e-cigs the most popular tobacco product for youths. A 2016 survey found that more than 20 million youths, or about four out of five middle and high school students, had seen at least one ad for e-cigarettes. The main source of e-cig advertising is retail stores, reaching 68 percent of youths according to the survey. Young people also saw ads online, on TV, and in newspapers and magazines. Some ads for

Vaping in Party Mode

Young people love Easter eggs, those hidden quirks or unexpected features added to a piece of computer software or a video game. Knowing their audience, Juul engineers included an Easter egg for their e-cigs: a special feature called party mode. To send a Juul device into party mode, a user takes a puff and waits for the LED light to go solid white. Then the user can wave the Juul around rapidly or slap it several times against the palm of the hand. The LED will begin cycling through a number of different colors—and the Juuler has something cool to show off to friends. Kids flock to social media to catch on to these latest wrinkles in the vaping scene. According to style reporter Lavanya Ramanathan, "On YouTube, just one blurry video showing you how to smack Juul into 'party mode' had more than 100,000 views."

Features like party mode also raise suspicions that Juul is not totally focused on the anti-smoking aspect of its devices. Party mode does not do much to help a longtime smoker quit cigarettes. But even adult vapers can have fun with a show of colored lights.

Lavanya Ramanathan, "We Killed the Cigarette. What We Got in Return Is Mango-Flavored Nicotine in 'Party Mode,'" *Washington Post*, August 8, 2018. www.washingtonpost.com.

One survey found that the main source of e-cigarette advertising is retail stores, reaching 68 percent of youths.

e-cigs include celebrity endorsements. Many highlight themes of style, freedom, and rebellion. For most kids, vaping is no mystery and, whether they participate or not, is regarded as a normal part of teenage life. Teens have become a natural customer base for an industry that publicly disavows their business.

The Juul Launch

When it comes to aggressive ad campaigns, the champion among e-cig makers has to be Juul. For its splashy product launch in 2015, the company—then called Pax Labs but known by its product name—spent more than a million dollars on Internet marketing. Moreover, instead of setting up a conventional marketing campaign, Juul decided to throw "a really great party" in New York City, as one former employee recalls. Guests, many of them young and photogenic, were urged to take selfies and blast them to social media accounts on Twitter and Instagram with the hashtag #LightsCameraVapor or #Vaporized. One widely shared image showed five young women with leather jackets and tattoos posing with their Juuls under the caption "Having way too much fun at the #JUUL launch party."[38] The company sponsored similar start-up parties in a handful of other cities, including Miami and Las Vegas. The party in Juul's hometown of San Francisco drew rave reviews on social media. Guests danced to a number of youth-oriented bands and received their own Juuls free of charge. They could even sample the powerful nicotine hits in special vapor lounges.

In fact, the company handed out more than five thousand samples at each of its early launch parties. When Juul executives learned that an FDA regulation made it illegal to distribute free samples of tobacco products, they began to charge party guests a fee of one dollar per vaporizer. The idea was to get Juuls in the hands of glamorous young people and then make sure their images went viral. The company kept up a hyperactive pace on social media to get the word out about this new, hipper version of smoking. For high school and middle school kids checking their phones, the Juul launch parties looked like the perfect mix of fun, style, and big-city sophistication. Soon they would be trying out Juuls themselves—not in a ballroom or convention center but in the restroom at school.

Deliberately Targeting Teens

Juul's Los Angeles–based advertising firm followed up on the parties with what company insiders call the Triangle Campaign. In a series of stylish ads online, on billboards, and in print media, young models flaunted their Juuls against a background of brightly colored triangles. Several ads featured teenaged women who appeared to be younger than eighteen, even though eighteen is the legal age for buying vaping products in most states. Some Twitter ads also focused on the product's sweet flavors. One touted pods for Juul labeled "Crème Brulee" and prompted viewers to retweet if they "enjoy dessert without the spoon."[39]

Researchers at Stanford University consider these ads to be obviously aimed at young people and even underage users. Robert Jackler, a Stanford physician, leads a team that has gathered thousands of e-mails, photos, videos, and social media posts that Juul used to launch and market its vaping products. Their collection forms part of a comprehensive look at the effects of tobacco advertising on young people. (Ironically, both Adam Bowen and

E-cigarette companies such as Juul advertise their products using models who resemble pop stars (like Ariana Grande) and other celebrities admired by young people.

James Monsees, Juul's cofounders, graduated from Stanford.) Jackler and his team also used the Internet Archive's Wayback Machine, an online storehouse of web pages, to recover old ad campaigns that Juul had scrubbed from its website to escape scrutiny. The trove includes more than 2,500 tweets and 400 posts on Facebook and Instagram.

Jackler notes how the ads and social media posts show a deliberate attempt to get teens interested in e-cigs. Attractive models, mostly young women in teen fashions like crop tops and ripped jeans, are shown dancing, flirting, and socializing while waving their flash-drive-size Juuls in the air. One ad featured a girl with a long ponytail in the style of pop star Ariana Grande. Instagram posts with tags like "Share Juul" depict young couples exhaling clouds of vapor face-to-face. There is no hint of using e-cigs strictly to quit smoking. Instead the ads hearken back to how tobacco companies used to attract young people to cigarettes with trendy approaches. "Juul's launch campaign was patently youth-oriented," asserts Jackler. "You started seeing viral peer-to-peer communication among teens who basically became brand ambassadors for Juul."[40]

The Influencers

These brand ambassadors are another key part of the marketing strategy employed by Juul and other e-cig companies. Known as influencers, they tout e-cigarettes to their own social group or, if they have a larger following via social media, to hundreds or even thousands of avid fans. In Juul's original marketing campaign, employees would e-mail young people who were first to try the devices, urging them to spread the word among their friends and acquaintances. "The initial person we had in mind was youngish, late 20s, early 30s, an influencer, someone who's affluent, an early adopter," says a former Juul employee.[41] The tactic helped make Juul a familiar brand among young adults and teenagers.

An Influencer for Juul

The Instagram photo has a relaxed, sexy vibe: A young woman stares into space as a puff of vapor from her e-cigarette rings her ruby lips. The tagline reads, "When smoking cigarettes is not an option, I've turned to @juulvapor. Read why, via the link in my bio!" Juul paid Christina Zayas of Brooklyn, New York, a thousand dollars for the post, which has since been deleted. Zayas, who is thirty-six years old, is a professional influencer, sharing her ideas on lifestyle and the latest consumer products with thousands of followers on Instagram and other social media platforms. According to Zayas, that particular Juul post reached nearly 4,500 viewers and received about 1,500 likes. "[Juul] liked my edgy style and that I appealed to the younger market," she says. Her post got lots of positive responses. "You make smoking look so good," wrote one viewer.

Influencers like Zayas have proved to be effective marketers for e-cigs, especially for youths swayed by appeals to style and whimsical humor. Stung by criticism about marketing to underage users, Juul ended its payments to influencers. Juul spokesperson Victoria Davis asserts that the program was informal and short-term, and the ten paid influencers were all smokers or former smokers age twenty-eight or older. Davis also claims that the audience for these social media leaders were of legal age for vaping. Nonetheless, Zayas admits that at least five percent of her followers are age thirteen to seventeen—the demographic that draws the most controversy.

Quoted in Michael Nedelman, Roni Selig, and Arman Azad, "#JUUL: How Social Media Hyped Nicotine for a New Generation," CNN, December 19, 2018. www.cnn.com.

Some influencers are virtual stars in their own right. Although Juul no longer pays directly for their endorsement, these professional influencers often get money from companies that sell their own versions of Juul pods, e-juices, or enhanced vaporizers. With their large groups of followers on Instagram, they can create buzz about e-cigs with each post. Some pass along images of friends juuling and doing tricks such as blowing double streams of smoke rings or manipulating a giant smoke ring with their lips. Selfies taken with Juuls emphasize images of relaxation, style, and sex appeal. Some posts hit the cultural jackpot, such as photos of pop star Katy Perry brandishing a Juul backstage at the

2016 Golden Globe awards. "What Juul did that's different is it exploited social media, where American middle and high school kids live," says Jackler. "That was their innovation."[42]

Marketing at Concerts and Festivals

E-cig companies also reach out to young customers at the places they like to party, such as music festivals, concerts, film events, and beach gatherings. On Memorial Day weekend in 2013, e-cig maker Blu sponsored the Sasquatch! Music Festival in Quincy, Washington. The company set up a vapor lounge where visitors could get sample e-cigarettes, use charging stations, and mingle with some of the festival's indie, rock, and hip-hop performers. In 2018 Juul was a sponsor for the Music in Film Summit at the Sundance Film Festival in Utah. Participants included actors Nicolas Cage and Elijah Wood, Black Eyed Peas member will.i.am, rapper KRS-One, and Dan Reynolds of Imagine Dragons. Festivalgoers were met with pavilions hawking Juul merchandise and paraphernalia. Although traditional cigarette and smokeless tobacco companies are forbidden by law from sponsoring sporting events and music festivals, e-cig makers face no such restrictions.

> "What Juul did that's different is it exploited social media, where American middle and high school kids live. That was their innovation."[42]
>
> —Robert Jackler, a Stanford physician who researches the effects of tobacco advertising on young people

Vaping companies are always looking for new ways to promote their wares to young people. Some have turned to offering college scholarships via essay contests for students. The required essay subject concerns the potential benefits of e-cigarettes versus smoking. These contests have helped land e-cig brands on the websites of prestigious universities. Many of the essay competitions have no age limit, allowing students younger than age eighteen to enter. Robin Koval, chief executive officer (CEO) and president of Truth Initiative, says kids are being lured with an anti-smoking message. "Most of these kids are not smokers," she observes. "What [e-cigarette manufacturers are] saying and what they're doing don't seem to agree here. But that's not surprising."[43]

Critics contend that e-cigarette companies have used fruit and candy flavors and aggressive social media campaigns to market their products to underage users. Since its buzzworthy 2015 launch with glamorous parties, Juul has spent large sums to expand its profile among young people. For its part, Juul continues to insist it does not target teenagers and mainly seeks to provide smokers with a less harmful alternative to tobacco. Laura Ellner, an influencer for the last decade, does not believe Juul aimed at the youth market, but some things are beyond the company's control. "Teenagers are going to be teenagers," she says. "Are we ever going to be able to stop kids from doing things they are not supposed to?"[44]

"Teenagers are going to be teenagers. Are we ever going to be able to stop kids from doing things they are not supposed to?"[44]

—Laura Ellner, an influencer for e-cigarette companies and other products

CHAPTER FIVE

The Crackdown on Teen Vaping

In November 2018 Juul, the wildly successful maker of e-cigarettes, announced it was taking major steps to reduce its appeal among underage users. Juul shut down its accounts on social media sites including Facebook and Instagram, where many teenagers get the latest info about fads like vaping. Stores were told to install ID scanners before they could resume sales of Juuls. The company set up an undercover "secret shoppers" program to check on illegal sales of their products at retailers.

Juul also stopped taking orders for kid-friendly flavors of its e-liquid pods, such as mango and crème brûlée, at the more than ninety-thousand retail outlets across the country that sell its products. Flavored liquids remained available on the company's website, but with added layers of technology to verify the age of buyers. Online customers have to provide their name, date of birth, home address, and social security number. In addition, to create an online account, buyers must use a security code sent to their cell phone and get a real-time photo matched to their uploaded photo ID.

Acknowledging Its Edgy Appeal

By making these moves to deter underage customers, Juul acknowledged its products' edgy appeal to teenagers and children—a popularity it claims never to have sought. "Our intent was never to have youth use JUUL products," says CEO

Kevin Burns. "But intent is not enough, the numbers are what matter, and the numbers tell us underage use of e-cigarette products is a problem. We must solve it."[45]

Some critics hailed Juul's proposals as a positive step to curb vaping among teens. However, others saw the moves as long overdue and unlikely to halt the alarming spread of e-cig use among youths. "Juul's announcement is too little, too late, and it's not a substitute for comprehensive FDA regulation of e-cigarettes," says Matthew Myers, president of the Campaign for Tobacco-Free Kids. "Now that it has become so popular with kids and captured 75 percent of the e-cigarette market, Juul can pull back on social media because its young customers are doing the social media marketing themselves."[46]

> "Juul's announcement [of steps to deter underage users] is too little, too late, and it's not a substitute for comprehensive FDA regulation of e-cigarettes."[46]
>
> —Matthew Myers, president of the Campaign for Tobacco-Free Kids

Myers and other activists are urging the government to crack down on sales and marketing of vaping products to underage users.

The FDA's Plan of Action

Observers were quick to note the likely reason for Juul's new guidelines. The company was responding to FDA commissioner Scott Gottlieb's November 2018 plan of action to curb sales of flavored e-liquids at retail sites such as supermarkets and convenience stores. Under the new rules, only menthol, mint, and tobacco flavors would be allowed for sale alongside unflavored e-cigs and standard cigarettes. In his proposal, Gottlieb stressed that flavors were crucial to the youth appeal of e-cigarettes like Juuls and others. This appeal led to a sharp increase in vaping among middle and high school students—more than 1.5 million new users in one year.

Around the same time, agents from the FDA made a surprise visit to the headquarters of Juul Labs in San Francisco, seizing a thousand pages of documents related to their vaping products. The agency gave five e-cig makers—Juul, British American Tobacco's Vuse, Altria's MarkTen, Imperial Brands' Blu, and Japan Tobacco's Logic—sixty days to submit detailed plans on how they intend to keep their vapes out of the hands of children. These brands represent 97 percent of the American market for e-cigs. Should the FDA decide the plans do not go far enough, the companies' products could be removed from the marketplace altogether.

In March 2019, Gottlieb issued a formal proposal outlining the FDA's new restrictions and enforcement efforts. Sales of flavored nicotine pods were limited to websites, tobacco shops, vape shops, and other retailers that would enforce age requirements

In November 2018, FDA commissioner Scott Gottlieb proposed steps to limit the sale of flavored e-liquids at retail sites such as supermarkets and convenience stores.

for buyers. Convenience stores and gas stations were required to have age-restricted areas to continue selling flavored e-liquids and pods. It was hoped this rule might remove vaping products from convenience store shelves altogether.

The Problem of Packaging

The FDA also promised strong efforts to keep companies from marketing e-cigarettes to minors. Gottlieb said the FDA might take action to ban all vaping products that are packaged to look

"The Real Cost" Campaign

In 2014 the FDA launched a campaign to inform young people about the dangers of smoking cigarettes. Called the "The Real Cost" campaign, it helped reduce underage use of tobacco products. Today the FDA is adapting its Real Cost effort to address vaping and the risks of nicotine addiction from using e-cigarettes. With so many young people getting hooked on e-cigs each year, FDA officials want teens to know that vaping is not simply inhaling a watery, fruit-flavored mist. Awareness is crucial, since nearly 80 percent of teens admit they see no great risk of harm from regular vaping. The campaign seeks to get the word out about how e-cigs can rewire youthful brains to instill a long-term craving for nicotine.

To reach teens where they live, The Real Cost Youth E-Cigarette Prevention Campaign delivers its message in schools and online. High schools and middle schools are provided with posters, handouts, and digital material. Posters can be displayed in school restrooms where so much surreptitious vaping takes place. Other anti-vaping materials are distributed to teachers and students through the educational publisher Scholastic and the organization Students Against Destructive Decisions. Ads for Real Cost are placed on social media sites and other digital platforms such as Hulu, Spotify, and YouTube. The FDA's Real Cost website includes videos and graphics that provide the facts about e-cigs. One video, titled *Don't Get Hacked by Vaping*, shows zombie-like kids with mouths shaped like USB adaptors hooking up to e-cigs. The FDA hopes teens will get the message and resist the vaping trend.

like juice boxes, candy, or cookies to entice children. Thirteen e-cig makers received FDA warnings about packaging aimed at minors. To press the point, the FDA issued a series of handouts that posed the question "E-liquid or food product?" The handouts showed how similar the packages for certain vaping liquids were to those for food items. For example, the multicolored box for an e-liquid called Candy King Sour Worms mimics the one for Trolli Sour Brite Crawlers, a gummy candy. The yellow package for V'Nilla Cookies & Milk e-liquid looks like the Nilla Wafers box. An e-liquid called Juice Box looks exactly like its name, and even has apples on the label.

FDA officials know such packages are magnets for youthful eyes. And while the bright colors and hints of delicious tastes get the kids' attention, the nicotine gets them hooked on vaping. "We think flavored products represent greater risk to youth appeal, so when we're looking at the public health value and redeeming qualities of products, we generally feel flavors have more to prove at this point," Gottlieb contends. "They're the ones driving youth use so we want to do a proper evaluation through our assessment process."[47]

Gottlieb, who left the FDA in April 2019, says he believes e-cigarettes should remain available to adults who want to stop smoking, but sales to minors must end. To further that goal, the government might require e-liquid flavor pods to get FDA clearance in order to remain on the market. "I think the marketability of pod-based products will be called into question if youth use rates continue to climb at the rates they're climbing,"[48] he states.

> "We think flavored products represent greater risk to youth appeal. . . . They're the ones driving youth use so we want to do a proper evaluation through our assessment process."[47]
>
> —Scott Gottlieb, former commissioner of the US Food and Drug Administration

Controversy over Bans on Flavored E-Cigs

Among tobacco-control experts, reactions to the FDA's crackdown on e-cigs ranged from skeptical to disappointed. Some critics were willing to give the new measures a chance but questioned how aggressively they would be enforced. Although anti-smoking and anti-nicotine groups welcomed the stronger focus on the vaping epidemic among American youth, many felt the new rules did not go far enough. Unless the feds came down hard on manufacturers and retailers, e-cigarette sales to minors would likely continue to rise. And many health professionals worry that teens who are lured into vaping with fruit and candy flavors are liable to become tobacco smokers. This could reverse years of progress in reducing the number of minors who smoke. "As young people become addicted to nicotine," says Jonathan Klein, a professor of pediatrics at the University of Illinois at Chicago, "they are more likely to become users of other tobacco products as well."[49] Robin Koval, CEO of Truth Initiative, favors a much more drastic regulatory approach to e-cigs. "Taking some flavors out of some stores and putting some of the flavors behind a curtain or in vape shops is not enough to protect young people," says Koval. "We urge the FDA to eliminate the flavors, not just to hide them behind a black curtain, and to eliminate online sales."[50]

E-cigarette companies counter that flavored e-liquids are important in helping adults quit smoking. They point to longtime smokers like Larry McLaughlin, a sixty-two-year-old construction worker who now puffs on mango-flavored nicotine pods instead of cigarettes. E-cig users like McLaughlin say the fruit flavors keep them from going back to the bitter taste of tobacco. The vaping industry also points to new research that indicates e-cigs have a real impact on smoking addiction. A 2018 study published in the *New England Journal of Medicine* found that 18 percent of e-cig users in a test group were able to go a full year without smoking, compared to 9.9 percent who used nicotine patches and other measures.

Some observers claim the FDA is being hypocritical in its assault on flavored e-cigarettes. They see traditional cigarettes as a much greater threat to young people. "There is absolutely no valid public health rationale behind prohibiting the sale of most e-cigarettes, but allowing the real toxic cigarettes to remain on the shelves," says Michael Siegel, a professor of community health sciences at the Boston University School of Public Health. "Although Juul use among youth clearly needs to be addressed, we have to be careful not to completely lose our sense of perspective. Smoking still kills more than 1,000 people every day. There is no evidence that vaping kills anyone."[51]

> "Although Juul use among youth clearly needs to be addressed, we have to be careful not to completely lose our sense of perspective. Smoking still kills more than 1,000 people every day. There is no evidence that vaping kills anyone."[51]
>
> —Michael Siegel, a professor of community health sciences at the Boston University School of Public Health

Health experts like Nancy Rigotti, a professor of medicine at Harvard Medical School and director of tobacco research at Massachusetts General Hospital, say more research needs to be done to determine whether e-cigs can help adults kick the tobacco habit. But Rigotti warns that bans on flavored e-liquids could interfere with adults' efforts to quit smoking. According to Rigotti, "We need to find out if Juul works for [quitting smoking], and if it does, we want to have it around but at the same time keep it out of the hands of kids."[52]

State and Local Controls on Vaping

Not content to wait for federal regulations, a number of states and cities have passed their own laws to control vaping. One strategy is to treat vaping the same as cigarette smoking. As of December 2018 twelve states and Washington, D.C., ban the use of e-cigarettes in all public spaces where smoking is already prohibited. Although the laws vary, most of these states ban vaping in schools, workplaces, childcare facilities, hospitals, arenas, and other indoor public spaces. Many cities post "No Smoking, No Vaping" signs where e-cig use is prohibited.

All fifty states have age restrictions on buying e-cigs and vaping products. California, Hawaii, Maine, New Jersey, and Oregon require purchasers to be at least twenty-one years of age. In Alabama, Alaska, and Utah, purchasers must be at least nineteen. In all other states, the legal age for purchase is eighteen. San Francisco became the first US city to ban sales of flavored e-liquids entirely. Experts vary on their views about age restrictions for purchasing e-cigs. Some believe they should be available to older teens as an aid to kick the smoking habit.

Some cities are joining with private attorneys to sue e-cig makers who market and sell vaping products to minors online. In November 2018 Chicago became the latest city to take action. Mayor Rahm Emanuel announced plans to file a lawsuit against eight e-cig companies caught selling products online to underage consumers. Similar actions are underway in Los Angeles and Philadelphia. The

A number of states and municipalities have passed laws prohibiting the use of e-cigarettes in schools, childcare facilities, hospitals, arenas, and other indoor public places.

Hard Times at the Groove-E-Juice Vape Shop

The wares in the Groove-E-Juice vape shop in Cuyahoga Falls, Ohio, have a cartoonish appeal. Rainbow-colored labels on the e-liquid bottles look like packaging for ice cream or candy. Flavors include the Berry White and Crunchy Munchy. "I use Ben and Jerry's [ice cream] as an inspiration," says shop owner Jason Nobles. "Tobacco flavors suck." Nobles himself switched from cigarettes to vaping several years ago, via his favorite strawberry-waffle e-juice. Now he sells his own fruity e-juice concoctions to vapers of all ages—although not underage ones. Customers can even choose the nicotine level in the e-liquids they purchase.

However, new FDA regulations on sales of e-cigs and liquids could threaten Nobles's livelihood. Exotic e-juices make up 90 percent of his business. Should the feds ban flavored e-liquids, Nobles's two vape shops might have to shut down. He claims to have already lost $10,000 in each of the last six months due to the new rules. Although Nobles checks IDs and posts warnings about age restrictions, he doubts the FDA's changes will solve the problem of underage vaping. "You can ban stuff all you want, that just makes a child to want something more," he says. "They will find a solution; they will find a way."

Quoted in Taeler De Haes, "Cuyahoga Falls Vape Shop Worried About FDA Restricting Fruity Flavors on E-Cigarettes," News 5 Cleveland, March 13, 2019. www.news5cleveland.com.

lawsuits are moving forward despite the FDA's announced crackdown on vaping companies and marketing to minors.

Mayors like Emanuel have grown impatient at what they see as federal foot-dragging on enforcement. "The FDA needs to get off their duff," says Emanuel. "I'm not sure any of us know what they're going to do. I'm not going to leave the health of our children to the FDA. We've seen a rise in e-cigarettes, and they've been twiddling their thumbs. This is under both (the Obama and Trump) administrations."[53] Emanuel directed Chicago health officials to send letters to thirty-three makers and retailers of e-cigs and e-juices. The letters requested information about the companies' marketing and sales practices, efforts to prevent use by minors, use of social media to promote vaping, product design, and policies for online sales. The mayor wants the companies put on alert that youth marketing of e-cigarettes will not be tolerated. "They said this product is about quitting [cigarettes]," Emanuel states. "You don't name a product after Jolly Rancher, you don't name a product after sex, if you're trying to quit. This was always about targeting, marketing and creating new addicts."[54]

An Increase in Vape Shops

Municipal health officials fear that new FDA rules could lead to many more stand-alone vape shops appearing in their cities. As the FDA cracks down on sales of e-cigs and vaping products in convenience stores and gas stations, retailers might seize the opportunity to set up independent shops to serve vaping customers. Officials question whether such shops will be diligent about checking customer IDs. "The FDA needs to go further," says Matthew Myers. "There is nothing to prevent the number of vape shops from rapidly expanding and there is no solid evidence that vape shops do a good job of preventing illegal underage sales."[55]

"The FDA needs to go further. There is nothing to prevent the number of vape shops from rapidly expanding and there is no solid evidence that vape shops do a good job of preventing illegal underage sales."[55]

—Matthew Myers, president of the Campaign for Tobacco-Free Kids

The FDA has tightened its rules on vape shops more than once. In 2016 it banned free samples, required e-liquids to be sold in childproof containers, and mandated warning labels on vaping products and ads. The FDA also required shops that blended their own e-juices to submit them for federal approval before offering them for sale. In addition many cities and towns required shops that sell e-cigs to obtain licenses or permits. Vape shop owners began to question whether they could stay in business, but most managed to survive. However, in 2018 the FDA renewed its scrutiny of retailers who sell e-cigs. An undercover

Some health officials worry that FDA rules limiting e-cigarette sales by retailers will lead to the opening of more vape shops, which might not take adequate steps to prevent sales to underage consumers.

investigation revealed many violations at convenience stores and independent vape shops. As a result more than 1,300 retailers received warnings and fines for illegal sales of vaping products to minors.

Andrew Osborne, owner of the Vapor Trail Shop in South Buffalo, New York, is not worried about enforcement of age restrictions at his store. The state recently raised the age for buying e-cigs to twenty-one. Osborne says most of his customers are former smokers in their forties. He is concerned, however, about a possible ban on flavored e-liquids. That, he says, could put him out of business.

As vaping among minors has risen dramatically, the FDA has taken steps to crack down on underage use of e-cigs. New rules designed to ensure that purchasers are of legal age have hit on-line retailers, convenience stores, gas stations, and vape shops. The FDA also has announced restrictions on sales of kid-friendly flavored e-liquids and vaping products with packaging aimed at enticing young users. Public health experts mostly applaud these efforts, but some caution that flavored e-cigs that help adult smokers quit should remain available. In the meantime, states and cities have also passed laws to regulate the sale and marketing of e-cigs. Concern over underage vaping continues to fuel attempts to restrict their availability across the nation.

Introduction: The Vaping Trend

1. Quoted in Angus Chen, "Teenagers Embrace JUUL, Saying It's Discreet Enough to Vape in Class," NPR, December 4, 2017. www.npr.org.
2. Quoted in John Daley, "He Started Vaping as a Teen and Now Says Habit Is 'Impossible to Let Go,'" NPR, June 7, 2018. www.npr.org.

Chapter One: The Basics of E-Cigarettes and Vaping

3. Quoted in Daniel J. DeNoon, "E-Cigarettes Under Fire," WebMD. www.webmd.com.
4. Quoted in Sarah Boseley, "Hon Lik Invented the E-Cigarette to Quit Smoking—but Now He's a Dual User," *Guardian* (US edition), June 9, 2015. www.theguardian.com.
5. Quoted in Kathleen Chaykowski, "The Disturbing Focus of Juul's Early Marketing Campaigns," *Forbes*, November 16, 2018. www.forbes.com.
6. Quoted in Martinne Geller, "E-Cigs a 'Consumer-Driven' Revolution Born from a Bad Dream," Reuters, June 9, 2015. www.reuters.com.
7. Quoted in HealthDay, "E-Cig Liquid Nicotine Containers Often Mislabeled," July 27, 2016. https://consumer.healthday.com.
8. Quoted in 41 KSHB Kansas City, "Bill Introduced That Would Ban Kid-Friendly E-Cigarette Flavors," March 4, 2019. www.kshb.com.
9. Quoted in Jayne O'Donnell, "FDA Declares Youth Vaping an Epidemic, Announces Investigation, New Enforcement," *USA Today*, September 12, 2018. www.usatoday.com.

10. Quoted in Kathleen Raven, "Your Teen Is Underestimating the Health Risks of Vaping," Yale Medicine, December 19, 2018. www.yalemedicine.org.

11. Anonymous testimonial, "Vaping Saved My Life," American Vaping Association. www.vaping.org.

12. Linda Richter, "Can E-Cigarettes Help You Quit Smoking?," Center on Addiction, October 2018. www.centeronaddiction .org.

Chapter Two: What Teens Are Saying About Vaping

13. Quoted in Danielle Grady, "V Is for Vaping: What You Don't Know About Your Teens' New Habit," *Leo Weekly* (Louisville, KY), November 28, 2018. www.leoweekly.com.

14. Quoted in Jia Tolentino, "The Promise of Vaping and the Rise of Juul," *New Yorker*, May 7, 2018. www.newyorker.com.

15. Quoted in Tolentino, "The Promise of Vaping and the Rise of Juul."

16. Dante Caloia, "Vaping an 'Epidemic,' Ottawa High School Student Says," CBC News Ottawa, December 21, 2018. www.cbc.ca.

17. Quoted in Hallie Cotnam, "Outside the School at West Carleton," audio file, CBC News Ottawa, December 21, 2018. www.cbc.ca.

18. Quoted in Lauren Levy, "New York Teens Created the Biggest Vape Trend (and Now They're Over It)," The Cut, April 18, 2018. www.thecut.com.

19. Quoted in Jan Hoffman, "The Price of Cool: A Teenager, a Juul, and Nicotine Addiction," *New York Times*, November 16, 2018. www.nytimes.com.

20. Quoted in Hoffman, "The Price of Cool."

21. Quoted in Hoffman, "The Price of Cool."

22. Quoted in Hoffman, "The Price of Cool."

23. Quoted in Hoffman, "The Price of Cool."

Chapter Three: What Is Everyone Worried About?

24. Quoted in Katherine Martinelli, "Teen Vaping: What You Need to Know," Child Mind Institute. https://childmind.org.

25. Quoted in Martinelli, "Teen Vaping."

26. Quoted in Martinelli, "Teen Vaping."

27. Quoted in Erin Brodwin, "We Just Got Our First Look at How Many Minors Are Using Silicon Valley's Favorite E-Cig, and It Doesn't Look Good," Business Insider, October 30, 2018. www.businessinsider.com.

28. Quoted in Brodwin, "We Just Got Our First Look at How Many Minors Are Using Silicon Valley's Favorite E-Cig, and It Doesn't Look Good."

29. Quoted in Michael Nedelman, "When Your Child Vapes, What's a Parent to Do?," CNN, January 11, 2019. www.cnn.com.

30. Quoted in Jennifer Fuentes-Tamu, "Does Vaping Prep Teens for Lifelong Addiction?," Futurity, August 25, 2015. www.futurity.org.

31. Quoted in Jayne O'Donnell, "Depression, Anxiety, Nicotine Withdrawal: Trying to Quit Vaping 'Was Hell,'" USA Today, December 27, 2018. www.usatoday.com.

32. Quoted in Raven, "Your Teen Is Underestimating the Health Risks of Vaping."

33. Quoted in Tara Haelle, "Teens Vaping E-Cigarettes Up to 7 Times More Likely to Smoke Later, but Not Vice Versa," Forbes, December 4, 2017. www.forbes.com.

34. Quoted in Nedelman, "When Your Child Vapes, What's a Parent to Do?"

Chapter Four: Do E-Cigarette Companies Target Teens?

35. Quoted in Jessica Lipscomb, "Juul's 'Action Plan' Is Too Late for Addicted Miami Teens, Mother Claims in Lawsuit," Miami New Times, November 15, 2018. www.miaminewtimes.com.

36. Quoted in Tara Haelle, "Public Health Experts on New FDA E-Cigarette Rules: It's Complicated," *Forbes*, November 16, 2018. www.forbes.com.

37. Gianna Delmonte, "E-Cig Marketing: Targeting Children or Epicurean Adults?," *VaporFi* (blog). www.vaporfi.com.

38. Quoted in Erin Brodwin, "Silicon Valley E-Cig Startup Juul 'Threw a Really Great Party' to Launch Its Devices, Which Experts Say Deliberately Targeted Youth," Business Insider, September 4, 2018. www.businessinsider.com.

39. Quoted in Erin Brodwin, "See How Juul Turned Teens into Influencers and Threw Buzzy Parties to Fuel Its Rise as Silicon's Valley's Favorite E-Cig Company," Business Insider, November 26, 2018. www.businessinsider.com.

40. Quoted in Brodwin, "See How Juul Turned Teens into Influencers and Threw Buzzy Parties to Fuel Its Rise as Silicon's Valley's Favorite E-Cig Company."

41. Quoted in Brodwin, "Silicon Valley E-Cig Startup Juul 'Threw a Really Great Party' to Launch Its Devices, Which Experts Say Deliberately Targeted Youth."

42. Quoted in Julia Belluz, "The Vape Company Juul Said It Doesn't Target Teens. Its Early Ads Tell a Different Story," Vox, January 25, 2019. www.vox.com.

43. Quoted in Truth Initiative, "4 Marketing Tactics E-Cigarette Companies Use to Target Youth," August 9, 2018. https://truthinitiative.org.

44. Quoted in Michael Nedelman, Roni Selig, and Arman Azad, "#JUUL: How Social Media Hyped Nicotine for a New Generation," CNN, December 19, 2018. www.cnn.com.

Chapter Five: The Crackdown on Teen Vaping

45. Quoted in Megan Cerullo, "Juul Says It Will Deactivate Social Media Accounts, Stop Selling Flavored Products to Retailers," *New York Daily News*, November 13, 2018. www.nydaily news.com.

46. Quoted in Kenzi Abou-Sabe and Rich Schapiro, "Juul to Remove Most of Its Flavored Products from Retail Stores," NBC News, November 13, 2018. www.nbcnews.com.

47. Quoted in Angelica LaVito, "FDA Outlines E-Cigarette Rules, Tightens Restrictions on Fruity Flavors to Try to Curb Teen Vaping," CNBC, March 13, 2019. www.cnbc.com.

48. Quoted in LaVito, "FDA Outlines E-Cigarette Rules, Tightens Restrictions on Fruity Flavors to Try to Curb Teen Vaping."

49. Quoted in Kevin Loria, "Use of E-Cigarettes Among Teens Is 'Exploding,'" Consumer Reports, February 13, 2019. www.consumerreports.org.

50. Quoted in Kevin Loria, "New Restrictions on E-Cigarettes: What You Should Know," Consumer Reports, March 15, 2019. www.consumerreports.com.

51. Quoted in Haelle, "Public Health Experts on New FDA E-Cigarette Rules."

52. Quoted in Angelica LaVito, "Juul E-Cigarettes Get a Bad Rap for Surge in Teen Use. But Some Adults Say the Fruity Flavors Help Them Quit Smoking," CNBC, November 2, 2018. www.cnbc.com.

53. Quoted in Aamer Madhani, "Cities Step Up Pressure on E-Cigarette Industry over Teen Vaping Epidemic," USA Today, November 13, 2018. www.usatoday.com.

54. Quoted in Madhani, "Cities Step Up Pressure on E-Cigarette Industry over Teen Vaping Epidemic."

55. Quoted in Oklahoma's News 4, "High School E-Cigarette Use Has Jumped Nearly 80%; FDA Wants New Regulations," November 15, 2018. https://kfor.com.

American Cancer Society
250 Williams St. NW
Atlanta, GA 30303
www.cancer.org

The mission of the American Cancer Society is to free the world from cancer. The organization funds and conducts research, shares expert information, supports patients, and spreads the word about prevention. Its website includes a large section on e-cigarettes, their health effects, and the problem of youth vaping.

American Lung Association
55 Wacker Dr., Suite 1150
Chicago, IL 60601
www.lung.org

The American Lung Association engages in research, education, and advocacy to improve air quality and beat lung cancer. The group's website includes a great deal of material on teen use of e-cigarettes, including articles like "E-Cigarettes, 'Vapes,' and JUULs: What Teens Should Know."

Consumer Advocates for Smoke-Free Alternatives Association (CASAA)
PO Box 2991
Plattsburgh, NY 12901
www.casaa.org

CASAA is a nonprofit group that seeks to educate the public and increase awareness about alternatives to smoking, including e-cigarettes. Its website includes a timeline of the history of e-cigarettes, news stories, scientific studies, and other informational materials relating to vaping products.

Mayo Clinic
200 First St. SW
Rochester, MN 55905
www.mayoclinic.org

The Mayo Clinic is involved in clinical practice, education, and research. As part of its focus on health care, the Mayo Clinic includes on its website information and research materials on e-cigarettes, such as "Vaping Health Risks for Teens" and "Are E-Cigarettes Safe?"

Parents Against Vaping E-Cigarettes (PAVe)
www.parentsagainstvaping.org

PAVe is a grassroots organization started by three mothers in White Plains, New York. The group's focus is on the dangers to young people's health from becoming addicted to the nicotine in e-cigarettes. They also want to convince the FDA to institute stronger regulations against the marketing and sales of e-cigarettes and flavored e-liquids.

The Real Cost
FDA Center for Tobacco Products
https://therealcost.betobaccofree.hhs.gov

The Real Cost website is part of the FDA's campaign to educate young people about the harmful effects of tobacco products, including e-cigarettes and e-liquids. The website includes videos and graphics that educate viewers about the dangers of vaping.

Truth Initiative
900 G St. NW, 4th Fl.
Washington, DC 20001
www.truthinitiative.org

Truth Initiative is the largest nonprofit public health organization dedicated to ending tobacco use. Truth Initiative engages in education, tobacco-control research and policy studies, community activism, and innovation in tobacco dependence treatment. Its website includes many articles on e-cigarettes and their addictive qualities.

Vaping Post

www.vapingpost.com

The *Vaping Post* is an online publication that provides information on vaping and e-cigarettes. It takes the position that e-cigarettes or vaporizers are a legitimate method for helping adult smokers quit. The website features articles and posts about the business, science, and politics of vaping.

Books

Elissa Bass, *E-Cigarettes: The Risks of Addictive Nicotine and Toxic Chemicals*. New York: Cavendish Square, 2016.

Kari A. Cornell, *E-Cigarettes and Their Dangers*. San Diego: BrightPoint, 2020.

eCigarettes (Pediatric Collections). Elk Grove Village, IL: American Academy of Pediatrics, 2017.

Sherri Mabry Gordon, *Everything You Need to Know About Smoking, Vaping, and Your Health*. New York: Rosen, 2019.

Carla Mooney, *Addicted to E-Cigarettes and Vaping*. San Diego: ReferencePoint, 2020.

Internet Sources

Erin Brodwin, "We Just Got Our First Look at How Many Minors Are Using Silicon Valley's Favorite E-Cig, and It Doesn't Look Good," Business Insider, October 30, 2018. www.business insider.com.

Jeffrey Buckley, "Vaping Laws: How Old Do You Need to Be to Vape?," *Vaping Daily Blog*, November 5, 2018. https://vapingdaily .com.

Kathleen Chaykowski, "The Disturbing Focus of Juul's Early Marketing Campaigns," *Forbes*, November 16, 2018. www.forbes .com.

John Daley, "He Started Vaping as a Teen and Now Says Habit Is 'Impossible to Let Go,'" NPR, June 7, 2018. https://www.npr .org.

Jan Hoffman, "The Price of Cool: A Teenager, a Juul, and Nicotine Addiction," *New York Times*, November 16, 2018. www.nytimes .com.

Angelica LaVito, "FDA Outlines E-Cigarette Rules, Tightens Restrictions on Fruity Flavors to Try to Curb Teen Vaping," CNBC, March 13, 2019. www.cnbc.com.

Michael Nedelman, Roni Selig, and Arman Azad, "#JUUL: How Social Media Hyped Nicotine for a New Generation," CNN, December 19, 2018. www.cnn.com.

Kathleen Raven, "Your Teen Is Underestimating the Health Risks of Vaping," Yale Medicine, December 19, 2018. www.yale medicine.org.

INDEX

PICTURE CREDITS